STEP-UP Books

are written especially for children who have outgrown beginning readers. In this exciting series:

- the words are harder (but not too hard)
- there's more text (but it's still in big print)
- there are plenty of illustrations (but the books aren't picture books)
- the subject matter has been carefully chosen to appeal to young readers who want to find out about the world around them. They'll love these informative and lively books.

WONDER WOMEN OF SPORTS

Kids will be amazed at how:

- Diana Nyad swam 60 miles
- Billie Jean King beat a male chauvinist pig at tennis
- Annie Peck climbed mountains at age 82
- Wilma Rudolph went from cripple to track star

In this collection of true stories about women athletes, young readers will also find out about:

- Nadia Comaneci, gymnastic superstar
- Babe Didrikson, the greatest woman athlete of the twentieth century
- Roberta Bingay, the first woman to run in the Boston Marathon

And more!

Wonder Women of Sports

by Betty Millsaps Jones

Step-Up Books ® Random House
New York

For Bruce and Brad

920
J

20,204

Photograph Credits: © Lyn Malone/The Image Bank, cover; Black Star, front endpaper; Brown Brothers, 19, 23, 56 (middle left, bottom left); Joan Chandler, 45; Culver Pictures Inc., 20; Focus on Sports Inc., 33, 34, 35; Photo Researchers, Inc., 15, 28, 29, 43; Pictorial Parade Inc., 51, 69; United Press International, 8, 11 (bottom), 13, 17, 18, 30, 31, 37, 40, 49, 54, 56 (top left and right, bottom middle and right), 61, 62, 65, 66, 67, back endpaper; Wide World Photos, Inc., 11 (top), 27, 42, 56 (middle right), 59.

Library of Congress Cataloging in Publication Data:
Jones, Betty Millsaps. Wonder women of sports. SUMMARY: Presents biographies of Wilma Rudolph, Mickey Wright, Nadia Comaneci, Billie Jean King, Annie Peck, Kitty O'Neil, Sonja Henie, Diana Nyad, Althea Gibson, Babe Didrikson, Roberta Bingay, and Joan Joyce. 1. Women athletes—Biography—Juvenile literature. [1. Athletes] I. Title. GV697.A1J66 796'.092'2 [B] [920] 80-20232 ISBN: 0-394-84475-0 (trade); 0-394-94475-5 (lib. bdg.)

Manufactured in the United States of America   1 2 3 4 5 6 7 8 9 0

Contents

A 60-Mile Swim

August 19, 1979. Diana Nyad set out to do something that had never been done. Could she swim to Florida from the Bahama Islands in the Atlantic Ocean? Could she swim 60 miles without stopping?

People told her that it was not possible.

Only two weeks before, Diana had tried. But she had to give up. She was stung by a sea animal called a Portuguese (pore-chuh-GEEZ) man-of-war. She cried when she was pulled from the water.

Diana had failed. But she was not going to quit. Today she was going to try again.

Diana began her swim before 5 a.m. Her body was covered with latex. Its milky liquid protected her from jellyfish stings. She wore goggles over her eyes. They kept out the salt water. She wore a few swimming caps on her head. They helped keep her warm.

Diana swam all day on the 19th of August. Her body hurt. Her lips and tongue began to swell from the ocean's salt. Diana tried to forget the pain. She counted her strokes. She sang songs. "Row, row, row your boat," she repeated over and over.

Some of Diana's friends followed her in a boat. They wanted to make sure that she was all right. Every few hours, they handed her something to drink.

The hours passed slowly. Ocean water keeps moving in currents. These currents pulled at Diana. Waves lifted her. Once, when a jellyfish stung her, she cried out, "Why? Why? Why?"

Day turned into night. Diana kept on swimming.

She was so tired. Strange pictures flashed through her mind. She saw things that happened to her as a child. She felt that she was watching them on a movie screen.

Night turned into day. Diana kept on swimming.

A few minutes after 8 a.m. on August 20, Diana reached Juno Beach, Florida.

Diana's friends keep an eye on her.

Hundreds of people stood on the beach. They cheered as she swam closer and closer to shore. People in boats waved to Diana. They blew whistles.

At last Diana's feet could touch the ocean floor. She rose from the water and waded ashore. A crowd of hundreds rushed to meet her.

Diana's left eye was swollen shut from the salt water. "My body feels like a train ran over me," she told the crowd.

But Diana was very happy. After swimming for 27 hours and 38 minutes, she had reached her goal. The distance from North Bimini Island in the Bahamas to Juno Beach is 60 miles. But during her swim, ocean currents had sometimes carried her backward. So Diana had swum much farther than 60 miles.

Diana spoke to the crowd: "Everyone said it couldn't be done." They yelled and clapped. They knew that Diana Nyad had just proven to the world that "everyone" was wrong.

Showdown at the Astrodome

The Astrodome is a large building in Houston, Texas. Baseball, football, and basketball games are played there.

On September 20, 1973, 30,000 people filled the Astrodome. Some paid as much as $100 for a ticket. They came to see the strangest tennis match ever played. They came to see Billie Jean King play Bobby Riggs.

Billie Jean King began playing tennis when she was 11. At 17, she was one of the best players in the world. In 1971, she became the first woman player to earn over $100,000 in one year.

In 1941, Bobby Riggs had been the world's best tennis player. Billie Jean was born two years later.

In 1973, Bobby Riggs was 55 years old.

BOBBY: "I can beat any woman!" BILLIE JEAN: "Hmpf!"

He still liked to play tennis. He also liked to clown around and play jokes. And he liked to brag.

Have you ever bet that you could beat someone with one hand tied behind your back? Bobby Riggs made bets like that. Once he played a tennis match holding a heavy suitcase in one hand. In another match, he held a dog on a leash while he played.

Billie Jean had won many championships. She was 25 years younger than Bobby Riggs. Even so, he said that Billie Jean could not beat him. He said that **no** woman could.

Many fans agreed. They thought that Bobby Riggs could beat Billie Jean badly. Billie Jean wanted to prove that they were wrong. She agreed to play.

Reporters wrote about Billie Jean and Bobby. Newspapers printed their pictures. They appeared on television. Soon, people all over the world began to take sides. Even people who had never seen a tennis match wanted to see them play.

At last the big night came. The players entered the stadium. The crowd went wild. Bands played. Billie Jean rode in a chair. It was carried by five handsome men. Bobby rode in a cart. It was pulled by six pretty women. The crowd cheered.

Before the game began, the players gave each other presents. Bobby Riggs gave Billie Jean a large candy sucker. The crowd laughed. Then Billie Jean uncovered her present for Bobby. She handed it to him. It was a baby pig! The crowd laughed harder.

The band stopped playing. The crowd grew quiet. The match began. Bobby took the lead. His fans went wild. When Billie Jean scored, her father jumped out of his seat. "Go, baby, go!" he screamed.

Billie Jean kept scoring. Her fans knew she was winning. "Bye, bye, Bobby," they yelled.

Two hours later, the match was over. Billie Jean had beaten Bobby.

September 20, 1973, was a great day for Billie Jean King. She had proved that Bobby Riggs was wrong. Millions of TV viewers in 36 countries had watched her win. And her prize for beating Bobby was $100,000.

Four Miles to the Top

Mountain climbers are tough. They have to be. They face great dangers. One slip—and they can fall thousands of feet to the earth below.

Annie Smith Peck was a teacher. But she wanted to be a mountain climber also. Annie's friends were horrified.

Why were they so upset? Because it was the 1890s. At that time, women were not even allowed to vote. People thought it was not ladylike to climb mountains.

But Annie wanted to climb. And no one was going to stop her.

In 1895, Annie traveled to Europe to climb the Swiss Alps. They are a group of very tall mountains. She climbed to the top of one called the Matterhorn. It is 14,692 feet (4,478 meters) high. Its sharp sides rise from the earth like a pyramid . Climbers have died trying to reach its top.

"Nothing to it," said Annie when she came down. She was 45 years old.

When Annie Peck was 58, she set out to do something that no one had ever done. She set out to climb Peru's Mount Huascaran (wahs-kah-RAHN). It is 22,205 feet (6,768 meters) high.

Mount Huascaran

Mount Huascaran has two high peaks. A valley between them is filled with a glacier (GLAY-shur). That is a huge body of ice. To reach the top of Huascaran, Annie Peck would first have to climb the glacier.

She knew that she could not do it alone. She hired two of Europe's best mountain-climbing guides. At first, everything went well. Then one of the guides became very sick. He had to stop climbing.

Annie and the other guide kept on. They moved slowly up the glacier. They did not want to fall. So they cut steps in the ice. And they carefully tested it for cracks hidden by snow.

After four days, they reached the top of the glacier. But they had not reached the top of Huascaran. Two thousand feet (610 meters) of rock were still above them.

On the fifth day, a strong wind began to blow. Annie and her guide grew colder and colder. They were in great danger.

Annie looked up at the mountain's peak. She was so close to the top. But she knew that they had to turn back. She was very sad. But they were too tired to climb in the wind. And they could freeze to death in its bitter cold.

Ten days later, Annie and the two guides started up Huascaran again. This time, it took three days to climb the glacier. Once again Annie was only 2,000 feet away from the top of the mountain.

On the fourth day, the three climbers moved very slowly. They headed for Huascaran's north peak. The wind was calm. But the air was very cold.

At last they reached the top of the mountain. Annie was very, very tired.

But she was happy. No one else had ever stood where Annie and her guides were standing. They had climbed one of the highest mountains in the world.

Still, one of the hardest parts was left. They had climbed up. Now they must climb down.

It was dark. Their food was frozen. Their hands were frostbitten. The three climbers kept slipping. Several times they nearly fell to their deaths.

Later, Annie said, "I was scared. But I said to myself, 'Accidents don't happen in my family.' And I went on down through the night."

In her honor, Peru named Huascaran's north peak Cumbre Ana Peck.

Twenty-four years later, Annie climbed her last mountain. It was New Hampshire's Mount Madison—5,363 feet (1,635 meters) high.

The amazing Annie Peck was 82 years old.

A Perfect Ten

In 1968 Nadia Comaneci (NAH-dee-uh com-mah-NEECH) was six years old. She lived in a small town in Romania. One day, a visitor came to her school. He watched the children playing in the schoolyard.

Nadia and a friend liked to pretend that they were gymnasts. They ran and jumped as they played.

The visitor was a famous gymnastic coach. He noticed Nadia and her friend. He watched them very carefully. When the bell rang, the two girls ran into the school.

The visitor tried to follow them. He thought that Nadia could become a very good gymnast. He wanted to coach her. But now he could not find her. She had disappeared.

The gymnastic coach went into all the classrooms. He wanted to find Nadia and her friend. He went into Nadia's kindergarten room. But he did not recognize her. He went back into all the rooms. He still could not find the girls that he had seen playing outside.

Then the gymnastic coach had an idea. He went back into the classrooms again. He asked, "Who loves gymnastics?" When he came into Nadia's room, she jumped up and waved her hand. The coach had found her at last.

Nadia began going to a special school for gymnasts. She had to work very hard. She practiced every day for four hours.

July 1976. Nadia was only 14. But she had become one of the best gymnasts in the world. Nadia flew from Romania to Montreal, Canada, to be in the Olympics.

Nadia on the parallel bars

The Olympic Games are the most important sports contests in the world. Each country sends its best runners and jumpers. It sends its best swimmers and ball players. Gymnasts, too.

The gymnasts perform for judges who watch them very closely. The judges watch to see how hard the moves are. They rate the gymnasts on how well they perform.

The highest score is ten (10.00).

But it is very, very hard to get a ten. Judges subtract points for mistakes. By 1976, hundreds of gymnasts had competed in the Olympics. Not one had ever earned a ten.

Nadia waited for her turn with the other gymnasts. She was restless. She walked around. She stretched her arms. She stretched her legs. She blew into her hands. She did back flips. She didn't seem to notice the other gymnasts performing on the floor.

Nadia on the balance beam

Or the crowd of thousands watching them.

Nadia's first event was the parallel bars. The two tall wooden bars stand side by side. One is nearly two feet higher than the other. Nadia swung from one bar to the other.

She twisted and turned, spinning through the air. Her body became a blur of arms

and legs. The crowd gasped. Nadia swung around and around the bars. Suddenly, Nadia let go of the bars. She soared through the air. She flung her arms high above her as she landed on the floor.

The crowd roared.

They knew that they had seen a great gymnast. Nadia waved to the crowd. She smiled. She knew that she had done well.

The crowd grew quiet. They waited for Nadia's scores. The five judges marked their scorecards. Suddenly, the score flashed on the scoreboard. Nadia's score read 1.00.

For a moment, the crowd was very, very quiet. Then, they burst into cheers. They knew that the score was wrong. The scoreboard could go no higher than 9.99. The judges had not given Nadia a 1.00. Nadia had scored a perfect 10.00.

In the 1976 Olympics, Nadia won three gold medals. And she scored not just one perfect ten. Nadia Comaneci scored **seven** perfect ten's!

Ten Birdies to Win

Mickey Wright shoots birdies and eagles. But Mickey Wright doesn't use guns. She uses golf clubs.

A golfer's aim is to hit a ball into a hole. Golfers count the number of times they swing their club at the ball. That is how they keep score. The lowest scorer wins.

Golfers try to score par. Par is a goal set for each hole. Par for a hole might be three.

Or it might be four or five. One swing, or stroke, less than par is called a birdie. Two strokes less than par is an eagle. Only a very, very good golfer shoots birdies and eagles.

November 13, 1964. Mickey Wright was in Midland, Texas. She was playing in the Tall City Open. The contest, or tournament (TOOR-nuh-ment), would last three days. Each day the players would shoot 18 holes of golf. Par for 18 holes was 71.

In the first days of the tournament, Mickey shot 73 and 72. Her total score was 145. The leader's score was only 135. Mickey was behind by 10 points. She was in eleventh place.

November 15. The last day of the tournament. Mickey had 18 more holes of golf to play. She thought that she could not win. But she would do her best.

Her first four holes of golf were amazing. She shot three birdies and one eagle.

And Mickey kept on playing great golf. She birdied the ninth hole. She birdied the tenth.

As she played, Mickey talked to herself. She kept saying: "One shot at a time. Work hard. Keep going."

The lowest woman's score on a course as long as the Tall City Open's was 64. Mickey wanted to break that record.

Mickey birdied the fourteenth. She birdied the seventeenth. The crowd grew more and more excited. But before each shot, they were very, very quiet. No one wanted to disturb Mickey.

When Mickey came to the eighteenth hole, her score was 58. It was the last hole. She was six strokes below the world record. Unless she made a horrible error, Mickey would break that record.

All along, Mickey had been thinking about the record. She had not thought about winning the tournament. She had been too far behind. Winning had not seemed possible.

But Mickey had played so well that she

had a chance to win. A woman named
Sherry Wheeler was in the lead. Mickey had
to shoot a par 4 on the last hole. Then she
would tie Sherry for first place.

Mickey was very careful. She didn't want
to lose now. Her fans held their breath as
she shot. One stroke. Two strokes. Three
strokes. At four, the ball went in the hole.
Mickey had shot the par 4! The crowd
clapped and clapped.

Mickey Wright's final score was 62. She had broken the record by two strokes. And she was tied for first place in the Tall City Open. How amazing! Mickey had started the day in eleventh place.

To break the tie, the two leaders entered a sudden-death playoff. They had to play until one player's score was lower than the other's. Sometimes it takes only one extra hole of golf to break a tie. Sometimes the golfers have to play many extra holes.

Mickey and Sherry both birdied the first hole. They were still tied. Then on the second hole, Mickey shot her tenth birdie of the day. Sherry could not match Mickey's score.

Mickey had won the Tall City Open. And she had played one of the greatest games in the history of golf.

Miracle in Rome

September 8, 1960. Wilma Rudolph stood in the Olympic Stadium in Rome, Italy. Just days before, Wilma had won two Olympic gold medals. It takes years of hard work to become an Olympic champion. But for Wilma, being in the Olympics was a miracle.

As a child, Wilma Rudolph could not walk. When she was four, she was very sick. First, she caught scarlet fever. Then she developed pneumonia (nooh-MOAN-yuh). Her mother and father were afraid that she would die. Doctors were able to save her life. But afterward Wilma could not move her left leg. The doctors said that she might never walk again.

Wilma's mother and father did not have much money. They could not afford to hire special nurses for Wilma. And they could not afford to buy toys and pretty clothes. But they gave Wilma lots of love. They never lost hope. "Wilma **will** walk again," her mother said.

One day each week, Wilma's mother didn't have to work. That day she and Wilma got up early. They rode a bus to a hospital four miles (more than six kilometers) away.

It was a long, hard trip for Wilma and her mother.

Slowly, very slowly, Wilma's leg began to get stronger. When she was six, doctors put a brace on her leg. Wilma tried to walk. She had to hop. She could not go very far.

Two years later, the doctors took the brace off her leg. Wilma limped. But she could walk! For three more years, Wilma had to wear special shoes.

Wilma had missed being able to run and play. Now she ran and ran.

Nine years later she was in the 1960 Olympics. Wilma had become a world champion. She came in first in the 100-meter race and the 200-meter race. She won two gold medals. On September 8, Wilma had a chance to win a third gold medal in the Olympics. Very few people have ever done that.

Wilma and her teammates

Wilma and three American teammates
would run the 400-meter relay. In a relay,
each runner runs only part of the race.
Wilma would run the last 100 meters.

The starting gun fired. Wilma's first
teammate leaped forward. In her hand, she
carried a stick called a baton. She had to
hand it to the next runner. She ran very
fast. She took the lead. She passed the

baton. Now the second runner raced down the track.

The third runner grabbed the baton. She sped toward Wilma. She reached out to hand Wilma the baton. Then the crowd gasped. The third runner had nearly dropped the baton.

The mistake slowed down the Americans. The runner from Germany ran right past Wilma. Wilma's team had lost its lead!

Wilma waited. She made sure that she grasped the baton in her hand. Then she sped forward. Her long legs looked like scissors moving back and forth. Her arms pumped up and down.

Years before her mother had told her: "Never give up. Never give up."

Wilma remembered. She ran faster and faster. And she came closer and closer to the girl from Germany.

Wilma neared the finish line. She leaned
forward. The crowd cheered wildly as
Wilma broke the tape.

Wilma had made up the lost time. Wilma
Rudolph had won her third gold medal.

Battle of the Superstars

It was a sunny day in 1962. The weather was ideal for a day at the ball park. At least, 18,000 people in Waterbury, Connecticut, thought so. They filled the ball park's stands.

They came to watch a softball game—a women's softball game. And they came to see a showdown between Joan Joyce and Ted Williams.

Ted Williams is one of baseball's all-time great hitters. He played for the Boston Red Sox for 19 years. For six of those years, his batting average was the highest in his league (leeg). (A league is a group of teams that play against each other.)

A baseball player's batting average shows how good a hitter he is. Anything over .300 is very good.

Ted Williams' lifetime batting average is .344. One year he batted .406. That's not just good. That's great! No baseball player since has come close to that.

Joan Joyce is a softball superstar. She has pitched more than 100 no-hit games. In them, not even one batter on the other teams was able to get a hit.

Joan Joyce's fastball zooms over the plate. It seems like a shot from a cannon. But could she strike out Ted Williams? Many people said no!

Soon the 18,000 fans were going to find out.

Ted Williams walked up to home plate. The crowd yelled and clapped.

Ted got ready for the first pitch.

Joan stood on the pitcher's mound. She stepped forward. Her right hand swung way back, high over her shoulder. Then suddenly her hand swung down to her leg. The ball snapped out of her hand. It zoomed over the plate.

Strike one. The crowd cheered.

The second pitch looked like an easy home-run ball. It sailed toward the batter at hip level. Ted Williams swung. But the ball curved upward. It went past his shoulder. Strike two.

The next pitch floated slowly toward the plate. But it wobbled. It moved up and down and from left to right. Ted Williams tried to hit the ball. He missed. Strike three. Ted Williams had struck out.

All together, Joan Joyce threw Ted Williams 40 pitches. Time after time, he swung and missed.

Finally, he had enough. He threw his bat down and walked away. The crowd went wild.

In the ten-minute show, Ted Williams got only one hit. The 18,000 fans stood and cheered as Joan left the pitcher's mound. She had met baseball's greatest hitter and won.

A Desert Rocket Ride

Kitty O'Neil lives dangerously. She has to. That's her job. Kitty is a Hollywood stunt woman. She has fallen 100 feet (30 meters) from a cliff. She has been covered with gasoline and then set on fire.

December 6, 1976. Kitty O'Neil stood in Oregon's Alvord Desert. Kitty was going to ride in a strange-looking car called the Motivator (MOE-tuh-vay-tur). It had only three wheels. Two were at the back. One was at the front. The car was very long and narrow. It looked like a rocket turned on its side.

The Motivator **was** a rocket—a rocket car. It had a rocket engine. But it was made to travel on land. Not in space.

Kitty had not come to Alvord Desert to make a movie. She had come to run a race against time. Her rocket-powered car could go very fast. Much, much faster than an ordinary car. Kitty wanted to break the women's land speed record. That was 308 miles (more than 495 kilometers) an hour.

Alvord Desert was perfect for Kitty's ride. It had 11 miles (more than 17 kilometers) of smooth flat ground. But Alvord Desert belongs to the United States Government. Kitty had to wait weeks to get special permission to ride there. She also had to get the owner of the Motivator to lend her his car. It was worth $350,000. He did not want to see it wrecked!

At last, Kitty was ready to race. Under the rules, she had to make two runs. First she had to go in one direction. Then she had to go back the other way.

Kitty climbed into the car. She weighed only 97 pounds (44 kilograms). But she had to squeeze herself into the tiny cockpit. That's where the driver sits.

The countdown began. Kitty watched as the count was signaled to her. "Ten . . . nine . . . eight . . . seven . . . six . . . five . . . four . . . three . . . two . . . one." Kitty pushed down the pedal.

Kitty prayed. The rocket's engine roared. Clouds of smoke poured from the back of the Motivator.

For a second, the car did not move. Then it zoomed down the desert. The rocket's roar shook the ground. The Motivator seemed to disappear. Thick clouds of smoke hid it. In 15 seconds, Kitty had traveled one mile.

Five seconds later, Kitty was going nearly 600 miles (965 kilometers) an hour. That's almost 11 times a freeway's speed limit. Many jet planes don't fly that fast.

In just a few more seconds, Kitty finished her first run. Her crew rushed to the Motivator. They made sure that it was ready for the second run.

Soon Kitty raced back across the desert. And she made it! Kitty broke the women's land speed record. She broke it by more than 200 miles (322 kilometers) an hour.

Kitty O'Neil is stunt woman for TV's Wonder Woman.

Her new record was nearly 513 miles (825 kilometers) an hour.

The roar of Kitty's rocket car had filled the desert. Her crew had cheered when they learned that she had broken the record.

But Kitty had not heard the rocket's roar. And she had not heard the cheers. For Kitty is deaf.

Being unable to hear has never stopped the daring Kitty O'Neil.

A Famous First

In Boston, the third Monday in April is a very special day. The Boston Marathon is held on this day. Runners from all over the world compete in the marathon. It was first held in 1897.

A marathon is a long contest. A foot race is one kind of marathon. It is a hard race. It is a very long race. It is more than 26 miles (42 kilometers) long.

Some runners do not finish the marathon. Their muscles cramp. They get blisters on their feet. They feel sick. Some faint.

Only one runner can be first. But every runner who finishes a marathon is very proud. Running in a marathon is that hard.

In 1966, Roberta Bingay wanted to run in the Boston Marathon. She rode a bus to Boston from her home in California.

Roberta traveled for four days. But she could not enter the race. She is a woman. Only men were allowed to enter.

Roberta had a plan.

She hid in the bushes near the starting line. When the race began, she jumped out and joined the other runners. She wore a sweatshirt with a hood. The hood covered her head. At first, no one noticed her.

Soon the sweatshirt was too warm. She took it off. Now she ran in a one-piece bathing suit and Bermuda shorts. Before long, people realized that a woman was running in the race.

Three hours and 21 minutes after the race started, Roberta reached the finish line. Four hundred fifteen men and Roberta began the race. She was the 124th runner to cross the finish line.

Roberta was very happy.

Now, no one could say that a woman was not strong enough to run in the Boston Marathon.

The next year another woman ran the marathon. She hid under a hood, too. More and more people began to ask this question. Why are women not allowed to run in the race? No one was able to give a good reason.

Finally, in 1972, the rules of the Boston Marathon were changed. Since then, hundreds of women have run in the race.

But Roberta Bingay was the first!

Roberta reads about herself in the paper. Her parents look on.

Athlete of the Century

Babe Didrikson was an amazing athlete. She was an All-American basketball player. She won two gold medals in track at the 1932 Olympic Games. She was a champion golfer.

She boxed. She bowled. She swam. She skated. She played baseball. She played football. She played tennis.

In 1950, newspaper writers honored Babe Didrikson. They named her the greatest woman athlete of the first half of the twentieth century. Here is one story that shows how great she was.

Babe was 18 years old in 1932. She worked for a big company in Dallas, Texas. The company had a women's basketball team. Babe was its star player.

High Jump

Swimming   **Baseball**

Javelin

Hurd

Golf   **Running**

Babe liked to play basketball. But she also liked to run, jump, and throw. So Babe asked the company to start a track team. Soon Babe was its star, too. The team practiced every day for two hours. At night Babe would practice by herself. She wanted to run faster than anyone else. She wanted to jump higher and throw farther, too.

July 16, 1932. Babe was in Evanston, Illinois. The company she worked for had sent her there. She was to run, jump, and throw against America's top track stars. The winners would go to the 1932 Olympic Games.

Babe entered eight of the meet's ten events. She set a world record in the high jump. She won first place in the shot put. (Throwing a heavy ball.) She was first in the long jump, too.

She set another world record in the
80-meter hurdles. She won the baseball
throw. She placed fourth in the discus
throw. And then she broke her third world
record of the day. That was in the javelin
throw.

With each new win, the crowd cheered
louder and louder.

At the end of the meet, Babe had won a
spot on the United States Olympic team.
And her company's team had won the meet.
They had 30 points. The second-place team
was 8 points behind. They had only 22.

The second-place team had 22 members.
But the winning team had only one
member—the amazing Babe Didrikson.
Babe had scored all of its 30 points by
herself!

Wonder Child on Ice

Wonder child. That's what newspaper reporters called Sonja (SOAN-yuh) Henie.

In January 1924, Sonja traveled to France from her home in Norway. She was Norway's figure-skating champion. She was going to try to win an Olympic gold medal for her country.

The other ice skaters wore long skirts. They wore black boots and stockings to cover their legs. People thought it was not ladylike for a woman's legs to show!

Sonja wore a mini-skirt. It was trimmed with white fur. She wore bright colors. But no one minded. Sonja was only 11 years old.

Sonja was tiny and blond. She looked like a doll on the ice. As she skated, Sonja smiled at the crowd. They loved her.

Sonja finished last. But everyone who saw her skate knew that Sonja Henie would be back. They knew that she could become one of the best skaters in the world.

February 15, 1936. The wonder child had grown up. Twelve years had passed since she had finished last. Now Sonja was in a small town in Germany for the 1936 Olympics.

In the 1928 and 1932 games, Sonja had finished first. Could she become the first woman to win three gold medals in figure skating?

Many people said no. They thought that a 15-year-old English girl would beat Sonja.

Eleven thousand people crowded into the Olympic ice stadium. Sonja skated onto the ice. There was dead silence.

Sonja smiled to the crowd. She had not lost a figure-skating contest in ten years. She knew that she could win today.

Still Sonja was nervous. The young English girl had skated first. And she had skated well. Sonja knew that she dared not make a mistake.

The judges nodded. The music began.

Sonja glided across the ice. She began to skate faster and faster. Then suddenly she leaped from the ice. Sonja spun through the air like a ballerina. She twisted around and around. The crowd clapped and clapped.

For five minutes, Sonja skated. At each move, the crowd cheered louder and louder. They knew that Sonja Henie had never skated better. Her jumps were higher than anyone else's. Her whirling spins were longer and faster. No skater could come close to beating her. The gold medal was hers.

Later that year, Sonja Henie won her tenth world championship. Afterward, she turned professional. She traveled the world in her own ice show. She even made movies.

Sonja won three gold medals and ten world championships. And she became a movie star. Young girls everywhere grew up wanting to be like Sonja Henie. But no figure skater has ever broken her amazing record.

Victory at Wimbledon

Football players dream of winning the Super Bowl. Baseball players dream of winning the World Series. Tennis players dream of winning at Wimbledon.

July 6, 1957. Althea Gibson stood on the Centre Court in Wimbledon, England. She had been playing there for two weeks. She had won match after match. She had made it to the final. Now she faced Darlene Hard in the championship match.

Only the world's best tennis players are invited to play at Wimbledon. Reaching Wimbledon is hard for most people. But it was even harder for Althea. You see, Althea is black. She had to fight for years to be accepted as a tennis player.

Althea Gibson and Darlene Hard

Althea's parents were very poor. They did not have enough money to buy Althea a tennis racket. And they surely could not pay for tennis lessons. Still, Althea became one of the superstars of tennis. Here is the story of Althea's long fight to reach the top.

Althea grew up in New York City. She and her friends played ball in the street. A city playground leader liked the way Althea played paddle tennis. He bought her a tennis racket. Soon she became a very good player.

One day Althea went with a friend to a black tennis club. Some members saw her play.

They wanted her to join the club. These members collected money to pay for her to join. And they gave her money to pay for tennis lessons.

Tennis players compete against one another in tournaments. They play a series of matches. Winners play winners. At the end, only one person has won all his or her matches.

Althea entered her first tournament when she was 15. She won easily. Before long, Althea had won many tournaments.

But just **how** good a player was Althea Gibson? No one knew for sure.

There were tournaments that Althea could not enter. She was good enough to play in them. But black people were kept out.

Althea knew that she was not being treated fairly. She was very sad. But she loved tennis. So she kept playing.

In 1950 a well-known white tennis player stood up for Althea. Her name was Alice Marble. Alice said Althea should be allowed to play anyone— white or black.

Alice Marble had won the United States championship. She had won at Wimbledon. Tennis fans loved and respected Alice Marble. They listened to her.

One month later, Althea was invited to play in Forest Hills, New York. The tournament was for the national championship. Althea was the first black person ever to enter.

Althea did not win. But she was happy to be there. And she came very close to beating the champion.

Seven years later, sixteen thousand fans filled the Wimbledon stands. They came to watch the biggest championship match in the world. Althea Gibson would play Darlene Hard. Just minutes before starting time, Queen Elizabeth entered the stands.

Althea quickly took the lead. The ball began to fly through the air faster and faster. Althea ran back and forth on the court. Darlene shook her head. She knew that she was losing.

In less than an hour, Althea had won the championship. Once, Althea was too poor to buy a tennis racket. Now she was the world's number-one player.

The 16,000 fans stood and cheered. Althea smiled and waved to them. "At last, at last," Althea whispered. She knew that she had proven how good a black player could be.

Now there was no doubt. Althea Gibson was the best.

Queen Elizabeth gives Althea her prize.

ABOUT THE AUTHOR

Betty Millsaps Jones is something of a wonder woman herself. She teaches English and is her school's Director of Guidance. She is also the mother of two active boys. Whenever she can, Mrs. Jones goes to see women's college basketball games. Somehow, she still finds time to write books and children's magazine articles! Mrs. Jones' favorite subject is women basketball players. Her book *Nancy Lieberman: Basketball's Lady Magic* was published in 1980. Mrs. Jones lives in Virginia Beach, Virginia.